JUST **4** THINGS

JUST **4** THINGS

Love Food™ is an imprint of
Parragon Books Ltd

Parragon
Queen Street House
4 Queen Street
Bath BA1 1HE, UK

Copyright © Parragon Books Ltd 2007

Love Food™ and the accompanying heart
device is a trademark of Parragon Books Ltd

Design: Terry Jeavons & Company
Photography: Mike Cooper
Home economist: Lincoln Jefferson

ISBN 978-1-4054-8780-1

Printed in China

This book uses imperial, metric, or US cup
measurements. Follow the same units of
measurement throughout; do not mix imperial
and metric. All spoon measurements are
level, unless otherwise stated: teaspoons
are assumed to be 5ml, and tablespoons
are assumed to be 15ml. Unless otherwise
stated, milk is assumed to be whole, eggs
and individual fruits such as bananas are
medium, and pepper is freshly ground
black pepper.

Recipes using raw or very lightly cooked eggs
should be avoided by children, the elderly,
pregnant women, convalescents, and anyone
suffering from an illness. Pregnant and
breast-feeding women are advised to avoid
eating peanuts and peanut products.

Contents

Introduction

For everyday eating, nothing beats home cooking for flavor, variety, nutrition, and cost. However, real life isn't like being a celebrity chef because you are the one who has to do all the shopping, preparation, cooking, and even cleaning up afterward, while trying to balance work and family life and, maybe, even squeezing in a few minutes of time for yourself. Buying the weekly groceries doesn't have to take the major part of your precious hours off, and preparing and cooking delicious, healthy meals doesn't have to be a time-consuming chore.

Using just four ingredients—excluding water, salt, pepper, any accompaniments, such as dipping sauces, or crispbreads, and optional garnishes—cuts down the amount of time you have to spend shopping and preparing food yet will still result in tasty and nutritious meals. As well as saving time—one of our rarest commodities nowadays—these recipes make choice easier. Many people find a long list of ingredients, followed by a mass of instructions, bewildering and even daunting, and it may be difficult to tell whether you'll like the dish once you've cooked it. If there are only four ingredients, you'll have a clear idea of what the characteristic flavor will be and even the inexperienced cook will be confident of success.

Perhaps the most surprising thing about the recipes in this book is the sheer variety of dishes you can create with just four ingredients. They range from great midweek family suppers to quick after-school snacks and light lunches, and from hearty stews, roasts, and bakes to impressively elegant dinner-party dishes. There is a chapter devoted to each course: Soups, Appetizers & Snacks; Fish & Seafood; Meat & Poultry; Vegetables & Vegetarian Dishes; and Desserts. Within each chapter, you'll find recipes to suit all tastes, occasions, and household budgets.

Using the best-quality ingredients is one of the keys to success with any kind of cooking, but it is perhaps especially important when there are only four of them. This doesn't necessarily mean that they have to cost more. Indeed, many of the recipes in this book are very economical. There are still

debates on whether organic ingredients taste better than conventional produce and you will have to make up your own mind about that. What is well established is that freshness is the star factor for flavor. Wherever possible, buy local and seasonal ingredients, which will taste better and will often retain more of their nutrients. Remember that flavor and aroma count for more than appearance.

1 Soups, Appetizers & Snacks

Homemade soups are always welcome, whether in a steaming bowl in winter or chilled for an alfresco lunch in summer, and the great thing is that they are very easy to make. This chapter also includes tempting snacks and appetizers that are great for both family meals and for entertaining.

Beef Consommé with Eggs and Parmesan

INGREDIENTS

serves 4

main

6⅓ cups beef consommé or beef stock

3 eggs

½ cup fresh white breadcrumbs

½ cup Parmesan cheese, freshly grated

pantry

salt

1 Pour the consommé or stock into a pan and heat gently, stirring occasionally.

2 Meanwhile, beat the eggs in a bowl until combined, then stir in the breadcrumbs and Parmesan. Season with salt.

3 As soon as the consommé or stock comes to a boil, add the egg mixture. When it floats to the surface, stir with a fork to break it up. Ladle into warmed soup bowls and then serve immediately.

Spinach & Cheese Soup

INGREDIENTS

main

8 oz/225 g fresh baby spinach leaves, tough stalks removed

2½ cups milk

3 cups vegetable or chicken stock

scant 1 cup Boursin or other cream cheese flavored with garlic and herbs

pantry

salt and pepper

croutons (optional)

serves ❻ to ❽

1 Put the spinach in a large pan and pour in the milk and stock. Bring to a boil, then reduce the heat and simmer gently for 12 minutes. Remove the pan from the heat and let cool completely.

2 Ladle the cold soup into a food processor, in batches if necessary, and process until smooth. Cut the cheese into chunks and add to the soup. Process again until smooth and creamy.

3 Pour the soup into a bowl and season with salt and pepper to taste. Cover with plastic wrap and let chill in the refrigerator for at least 3 hours. Stir well before ladling into bowls. Add croutons, if using, and serve immediately.

Easy Asparagus Soup

INGREDIENTS

main

15 oz/425 g canned asparagus spears

2 tbsp butter

2 tbsp all-purpose flour

2½ cups milk

pantry

salt and pepper

serves ❹

1 Drain the asparagus, reserving the can juices. Cut the asparagus spears into short lengths and set aside.

2 Melt the butter in a pan over low heat. Stir in the flour and cook, stirring continuously, for 1 minute. Remove the pan from the heat.

3 Gradually stir in the reserved can juices, then slowly stir in the milk. Return the pan to the heat and bring to a boil, stirring continuously. Add the asparagus spears and heat through gently for 2 to 3 minutes.

4 Remove the pan from the heat and let cool slightly, then ladle the soup into a food processor, in batches if necessary, and process until smooth. Stir well before ladling into bowls. Season with salt and pepper, to taste, and serve.

Cream of Pea Soup

INGREDIENTS

main

8 tbsp butter

1 onion, finely chopped

1 lb/450 g shelled peas

2½–3 cups milk

pantry

½ cup water

salt and pepper

serves ❹

1 Melt the butter in a pan over low heat. Add the onion and cook, stirring occasionally, for 5 minutes until softened.

2 Add the peas and pour in the water. Increase the heat to medium and simmer for 3 to 4 minutes, or until the peas are tender. (Frozen peas will be ready in 10 minutes.)

3 Add 2½ cups of the milk, season with salt and pepper, and then bring to a boil, stirring continuously.

4 Remove the pan from the heat and let cool slightly, then pour the soup into a food processor and process to a smooth purée.

5 Return the soup to the rinsed-out pan and bring back to a boil. If the soup seems too thick, heat the remaining milk in a small pan and stir it into the soup. Taste and adjust the seasoning if necessary, and serve.

Leek & Potato Soup

INGREDIENTS

main

4 tbsp butter

4 leeks, trimmed and chopped

12 oz/350 g potatoes, diced

3½ cups chicken or vegetable stock

pantry

salt and pepper

extra virgin olive oil, for drizzling (optional)

serves ④

1 Melt half the butter in a pan over low heat. Add the leeks and cook, stirring occasionally, for 5 minutes until softened.

2 Add the potatoes and cook, stirring occasionally, for 3 minutes. Increase the heat to medium, pour in the stock, and bring to a boil. Reduce the heat, cover, and simmer for 35 to 40 minutes, or until the leeks and potatoes are tender.

3 Remove the pan from the heat and stir in the remaining butter in small pieces at a time. Season with salt and pepper to taste. Press the soup through a strainer or pass through a food mill into a warmed bowl. Alternatively, ladle the soup straight into a bowl to leave it with a chunky texture. Serve immediately, drizzled with extra virgin olive oil, if using.

Chilled Avocado Soup

INGREDIENTS

main

4 cups chicken or vegetable stock

1 cup heavy cream

2 large avocados

2 tbsp finely chopped fresh chives

pantry

salt and pepper

Tabasco sauce (optional)

serves 4

1 Pour the stock and cream into a pan and bring to just below boiling point over low heat.

2 Halve the avocados and remove the pits. Using a fork, mash the flesh in the half shells, then scoop out into a bowl. Pour the stock mixture into the mashed avocado, whisking continuously with a balloon whisk.

3 Season with salt and pepper to taste and let cool, then cover with plastic wrap and chill in the refrigerator for 2 to 3 hours. Stir the soup and serve sprinkled with the chives and dotted with Tabasco sauce, if using.

Chilled Red Pepper & Orange Soup

INGREDIENTS

main

5 blood oranges

3 tbsp olive oil

3½ lb/1.5 kg red bell peppers, seeded and sliced

1½ tbsp orange flower water

pantry

salt and pepper

extra virgin olive oil, for drizzling (optional)

serves ❹

1 Finely grate the rind of one of the oranges and shred the rind of another with a citrus zester. Set aside. Squeeze the juice from all the oranges.

2 Heat the oil in a pan, add the red bell peppers and cook over medium heat, stirring occasionally, for 10 minutes. Stir in the grated orange rind and cook for an additional few minutes. Reduce the heat, cover, and simmer gently, stirring occasionally, for 20 minutes.

3 Remove the pan from the heat, let cool slightly, then transfer the red pepper mixture to a food processor and process to a smooth purée. Add the orange juice and orange flower water and process again until thoroughly combined.

4 Transfer the soup to a bowl, season with salt and pepper to taste, and let cool completely, then cover with plastic wrap and chill in the refrigerator for 3 hours. Stir well before serving sprinkled with the shredded orange rind and drizzled with extra virgin olive oil, if using.

Bacon Rolls

INGREDIENTS

main

9 baby leeks

9 thin slices of lean Canadian bacon

1 tbsp cornstarch

1½ tbsp sunflower oil

pantry

salt and pepper

serves ❹

1 Trim the baby leeks to the same length, then blanch in a pan of salted boiling water for 2 minutes. Drain and refresh in cold water, then drain again.

2 Put 3 slices of bacon side by side on a clean counter, overlapping them slightly. Brush lightly with a little cornstarch. Place 3 leeks, alternating the bulb and leaf ends, at one end of the bacon and roll up securely. Tie with kitchen string. Repeat with the remaining bacon, cornstarch, and leeks.

3 Heat the oil in a skillet, add the bacon rolls, and cook over medium-low heat, turning frequently, for 6 to 8 minutes until the bacon is cooked through and lightly colored.

4 Remove the rolls with a slotted spoon and drain on paper towels. Remove and discard the string and cut the rolls into slices about ½ inch/1 cm thick. Arrange in a warmed dish, season with pepper, and serve immediately.

Ham & Asparagus Rolls

INGREDIENTS

main

6 large slices cooked ham

15 oz/425 g canned asparagus spears, drained

1¼ cups condensed asparagus or mushroom soup

5 oz/140 g Gruyère cheese, grated

serves ❻

1 Preheat the oven to 350°F/180°C. Spread out the slices of ham and divide the asparagus spears among them. Roll up the ham to wrap around the spears and put the rolls in an ovenproof dish.

2 Pour the condensed soup into a pan and heat gently, without adding any extra liquid, but do not allow it to boil. When the soup is hot, remove the pan from the heat and stir in the grated cheese until melted.

3 Pour the soup over the ham rolls and bake for 20 minutes, or until hot and bubbling. Serve immediately straight from the dish.

Chorizo with Parsley & Olives

INGREDIENTS

main

1½ lb/650 g chorizo sausage, cut into ¼-inch/ 5-mm slices

1 tbsp olive oil

bunch of fresh flat-leaf parsley, chopped

½ cup black olives

serves 6

1 Heat a large, heavy-bottom skillet, add the chorizo slices, and cook over medium heat, turning and stirring frequently, for 5 minutes until crisp. Remove from the skillet with a spatula and drain well on paper towels. Discard the fat remaining in the skillet.

2 Heat the oil in the skillet, add the cooked chorizo slices, parsley, and olives, and cook, stirring continuously, for 3 to 4 minutes, or until heated through. Serve immediately.

Tomato Bruschetta

INGREDIENTS

main

8 slices of rustic bread

4 garlic cloves, halved

8 plum tomatoes, peeled and diced

extra virgin olive oil, for drizzling

pantry

salt and pepper

fresh basil leaves, to garnish (optional)

serves 4

1 Preheat the broiler. Lightly toast the bread on both sides. Rub each piece of toast with half a garlic clove and then return to the broiler for a few seconds.

2 Divide the diced tomatoes among the toasts. Season with salt and pepper to taste and drizzle with olive oil. Serve immediately, garnished with basil leaves, if using.

Nachos with Chiles & Olives

INGREDIENTS

main

2 lb/1 kg tortilla chips

6 tbsp chopped pickled jalapeño chiles

2/3 cup black olives, pitted and sliced

1 lb/450 g cheddar cheese, grated

pantry

dipping sauce

serves 4

1 Preheat the oven to 350°F/180°C. Spread out the tortilla chips in a large ovenproof dish.

2 Sprinkle the chiles, olives, and grated cheese evenly over the tortilla chips and bake for 12 to 15 minutes, or until the cheese is melted and bubbling. Serve immediately with a dipping sauce of your choice.

Eggplant Pâté

INGREDIENTS

serves 4 to 6

main

2 large eggplants

4 tbsp extra virgin olive oil

2 garlic cloves, very finely chopped

4 tbsp lemon juice

pantry

salt and pepper

6 crispbreads

1 Preheat the oven to 350°F/180°C. Score the skins of the eggplants with the point of a sharp knife, without piercing the flesh, and place them on a baking sheet. Bake for 1¼ hours, or until soft.

2 Remove the eggplants from the oven and leave until cool enough to handle. Cut them in half and, using a spoon, scoop out the flesh into a bowl. Mash the flesh thoroughly.

3 Gradually beat in the olive oil then stir in the garlic and lemon juice. Season with salt and pepper to taste. Cover with plastic wrap and store in the refrigerator until required. Serve with the crispbreads.

Artichokes with Parsley Butter

INGREDIENTS

main

4 globe artichokes

8 tbsp butter

2 garlic cloves, finely chopped

2 tbsp chopped fresh flat-leaf parsley

pantry

salt

serves ❹

1 Break off the stems of the artichokes and cut off the top ½ inch/1 cm of the head with a sharp knife. Using kitchen scissors, cut off the points of the remaining leaves.

2 Put the artichokes in a pan and add water to cover and a pinch of salt. Bring to a boil, then reduce the heat, cover, and simmer for 45 minutes, or until cooked. Test by gently pulling a lower leaf. If it comes away easily, the artichoke is ready. Drain well and place upside down on paper towels.

3 Melt the butter in a small pan over low heat. Add the garlic and cook, stirring continuously, for 30 seconds. Remove the pan from the heat and stir in the parsley. Pour the herb butter into a small serving bowl. Place the artichokes, right way up, on serving plates and serve with the butter.

2 Fish & Seafood

Fish is invariably at its best when cooked
simply with complementary rather than
overpowering flavors, so it's the perfect
choice for discovering the versatility
of using just four ingredients. From
Japanese-style tuna to family bakes,
and from spicy shrimp to creamy mussels,
you will be spoilt for choice.

Flounder in Cream Sauce

INGREDIENTS

serves 4

main

1¾ lb/800 g flounder fillets

4 tbsp butter, melted

1 cup sour cream

2 oz/55 g cheddar cheese, grated

pantry

salt and pepper

chopped fresh parsley, to garnish (optional)

1 Preheat the broiler. If the flounder fillets have not already been skinned, you can do this yourself if you prefer. Anchor a fillet to a cutting board with a little salt. Insert the blade of a sharp knife at the tail end and then, holding the skin securely and with the knife blade at an angle, gradually cut the fillet away from the skin with a sawing motion. Repeat with the remaining fillets.

2 Brush the tops of the fillets with melted butter and cook under the broiler for 6 minutes. Remove the broiler pan and spread each fillet with sour cream and sprinkle evenly with the grated cheese.

3 Return the fish to the broiler and cook for 1 to 2 minutes, or until the cheese has melted. Serve immediately, seasoned with pepper and garnished with chopped parsley, if using.

Baked Snapper

INGREDIENTS

main

2 bunches fresh basil

6 tbsp unsalted butter, softened

4 garlic cloves, crushed

4 red snapper, about 12 oz/350 g each, scaled, trimmed, and cleaned

pantry

salt and pepper

serves ❹

1 Preheat the oven to 350°F/180°C. Cut out 4 double thickness squares of foil each large enough to hold a whole fish.

2 Chop the basil leaves. Cream the butter in a bowl with a wooden spoon, then beat in the chopped basil and the garlic.

3 Season the fish inside and out with salt and pepper. Put a fish on a double thickness square of foil. Spoon one-quarter of the basil and garlic butter into the cavity and wrap the foil around the fish to enclose it completely. Repeat with the remaining fish.

4 Put the fish parcels on a large baking sheet and bake for 25 to 30 minutes, or until the fish flakes easily when tested with the point of a knife. Transfer the fish parcels to warmed plates and unwrap. Carefully slide out the fish and the cooking juices onto the plates, and serve immediately.

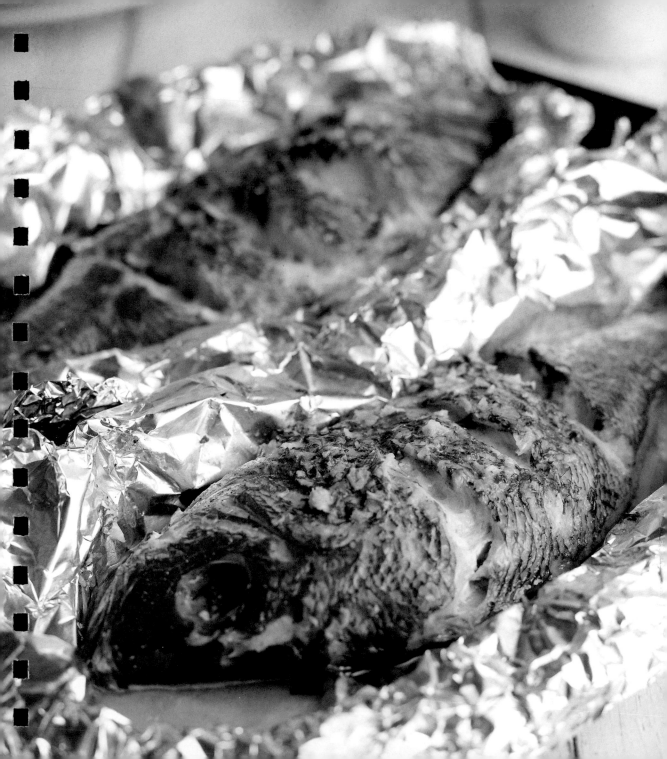

Oven-Baked Swordfish Steaks

INGREDIENTS

main

**4 swordfish steaks, about
7 oz/200 g each**

2 lemons or 3 limes

4 tbsp butter

8 canned artichoke hearts

pantry

salt and pepper

serves 4

1 Preheat the oven to 350°F/180°C. Cut out
4 double thickness squares of foil, each large
enough to hold the fish steaks.

2 Put a fish steak on each of the squares and
fold up the sides until partly enclosed. Season
with salt and pepper. Squeeze the juice from
1 of the lemons or 1½ of the limes. Cut the
butter into quarters and place a quarter on
each piece of fish. Top each steak with
2 artichoke hearts and divide the juice
among the parcels.

3 Fold over the foil to seal in the juice, and put
the parcels on a large baking sheet. Bake for
25 minutes, or until the flesh flakes easily when
tested with the point of a knife.

4 Meanwhile, slice the remaining lemon or
limes. Transfer the fish parcels to warmed
serving plates, open the tops, and garnish with
the lemon or lime slices. Serve immediately.

Salmon & Cheese Wraps

INGREDIENTS

main

**4 salmon fillets, about
7 oz/200 g each**

**4 slices of Taleggio cheese,
rind removed**

8 fresh sage leaves

8 slices of prosciutto

pantry

salt and pepper

extra virgin olive oil, for drizzling
(optional)

serves 4

1 Season the fish with salt and pepper. Cut the cheese slices to fit the top of the salmon fillets and place them on the fish. Put 2 sage leaves on top of each cheese-topped fillet, then wrap each fillet in 2 slices of prosciutto.

2 Heat a ridged grill pan. Add the wrapped fish fillets and cook over medium heat for 5 minutes. Using a spatula, carefully turn over each fillet and cook for an additional 5 minutes.

3 Transfer the wrapped salmon fillets to warmed serving plates. Serve immediately, drizzled with extra virgin olive oil, if using.

Salmon & Herbs in Prosciutto Parcels

INGREDIENTS

serves 4

main

2 bunches of mixed fresh herbs, such as cilantro, parsley, basil, and dill

½–¾ cup extra virgin olive oil

4 salmon fillets, about 7 oz/200 g each

8 slices of prosciutto

pantry

salt and pepper

1 Preheat the oven to 350°F/180°C. Coarsely chop the mixed herbs and put in a mortar, season with a little salt, and pound with a pestle. Gradually work in the olive oil to make a thick paste.

2 Spread the herb paste evenly over the tops of the salmon fillets, then wrap each fillet in 2 slices of prosciutto.

3 Put the wrapped fillets on a large baking sheet and bake for 20 to 25 minutes. Transfer to warmed serving plates and serve immediately.

Sole with Mushrooms

INGREDIENTS

main

6 tbsp unsalted butter, plus extra for greasing

8 sole fillets, about 3 oz/85 g each

juice of 1 lemon

4 oz/115 g chanterelle mushrooms, torn into thin strips

pantry

salt and pepper

serves ❹

1 Preheat the oven to 375°F/190°C. Grease an ovenproof dish with butter.

2 Season the fish fillets with salt and pepper, spread the tops with half the butter, and sprinkle with the lemon juice. Put 4 fillets in the prepared dish and top with an even layer of mushrooms. Place the remaining fillets on top and dot with the remaining butter.

3 Cover the dish with a lid or sheet of foil, put on a baking sheet, and bake for 20 minutes, or until the flesh flakes easily when tested with the point of a knife. Serve immediately, straight from the dish.

Marinated Monkfish Kabobs

INGREDIENTS

main

¼ cup olive oil

2 tbsp lemon juice

1½ tsp chopped fresh marjoram or oregano

1½ lb/550 g monkfish fillet, cut into 1-inch/2.5-cm cubes

pantry

salt and pepper

serves ❹

1 Mix the oil, lemon juice, and marjoram together in a nonmetallic dish and season with salt and pepper. Add the monkfish cubes and turn to coat. Let marinate for 30 minutes.

2 Preheat the broiler. Drain the monkfish and thread the cubes onto 8 presoaked wooden skewers. Place under the broiler and cook, turning frequently, for 3 to 5 minutes, or until the flesh flakes easily when tested with the point of a knife. Serve immediately.

Swordfish with a Crisp Tomato Topping

INGREDIENTS

main

4 swordfish or tuna steaks, about 6 oz/175 g each

3 tomatoes, sliced

1½ cups fresh whole wheat breadcrumbs

grated rind and juice of 1½ lemons

pantry

pepper

lemon wedges (optional)

serves 4

1 Preheat the oven to 400°F/200°C. Arrange the fish steaks in an ovenproof dish in a single layer and cover with the tomato slices.

2 Mix the breadcrumbs with the lemon rind and juice in a bowl and spoon the mixture evenly over the tomatoes.

3 Place the dish on a baking sheet and bake for 20 to 25 minutes, or until the fish flakes easily when tested with the point of a knife. Serve immediately straight from the dish, seasoned with pepper, and garnished with lemon wedges, if using.

Skate with Caper Berries

INGREDIENTS

serves **4**

main

**4 skate wings, about
8 oz/225 g each, skinned
and trimmed**

1½ tbsp olive oil

**3 tbsp caper berries or
capers, rinsed**

**grated rind and juice of
1 orange**

pantry

salt and pepper

1 Heat a ridged grill pan. Pat the skate wings dry with paper towels. Brush both sides of the skate wings with the oil, add to the pan, and cook over high heat for 3 to 4 minutes on each side, depending on the thickness of the wings.

2 Reduce the heat and sprinkle the fish with the caper berries, orange rind, and juice. Cook for an additional 1 minute and season with salt and pepper to taste. Serve immediately.

Teriyaki Tuna

INGREDIENTS

main

**4 tuna steaks, about
6 oz/175 g each**

6 tbsp sake

6 tbsp mirin

**6 tbsp shoyu (Japanese
soy sauce)**

serves ❹

1 Arrange the tuna steaks in a single layer in a shallow dish. Mix the sake, mirin, and shoyu together in a pitcher. Pour the mixture over the fish, turning to coat, then cover with plastic wrap and let marinate in the refrigerator for 6 to 8 hours.

2 Preheat the broiler. Drain the tuna, reserving the marinade. Put the fish on a broiler rack and cook, brushing frequently with the reserved marinade, for 2 to 4 minutes on each side, depending on how well done you like your tuna. Alternatively, you can cook the fish on a barbecue.

3 Pour any remaining marinade into a small pan and bring just to a boil, then remove the pan from the heat. Serve the tuna hot with the warmed sauce.

Baked Fish with Preserved Lemons

INGREDIENTS

main

1 sea bream or sea bass, about 3½ lb/1.5 kg, trimmed, scaled, and cleaned

2 tbsp chopped fresh cilantro

1 tbsp sweet paprika

large jar of lemon slices, preserved in oil

pantry

salt and pepper

serves ❹

1 Preheat the oven to 475°F/240°C. Using a sharp knife, slash the fish diagonally 3 to 4 times on each side. Season the fish inside and out with salt and pepper. Put the cilantro in the cavity and rub the paprika all over the outside of the fish.

2 Drain about 20 lemon slices and put 10 to 12 in the base of an ovenproof dish large enough to hold the fish. Place the fish on top and cover with the remaining drained lemon slices. Measure ⅔ cup of the oil from the jar of lemons and pour it over the fish.

3 Put the dish on a large baking sheet and bake for 5 minutes, then reduce the oven temperature to 350°F/180°C and bake, basting frequently, for an additional 40 to 45 minutes, or until the flesh flakes easily when tested with the point of a knife. Serve immediately straight from the dish.

Sea Bream with Tomatoes, Yogurt & Spinach

INGREDIENTS

main

1½ lb/650 g fresh spinach leaves, tough stalks removed

6 sea bream fillets, about 6 oz/175 g each

6 tbsp strained plain yogurt

6 tomatoes, peeled, seeded, and diced

pantry

salt and pepper

extra virgin olive oil, for drizzling (optional)

serves 6

1 Preheat the oven to 450°F/230°C. Blanch the spinach in a pan of salted boiling water for 1 minute. Drain well, squeezing out as much liquid as possible, and pat dry with paper towels. Set aside.

2 Season the fish fillets with salt and pepper. Arrange overlapping spinach leaves into 6 sheets large enough to enclose a fillet. Place a fillet on each spinach sheet and spoon 1 tablespoon of yogurt on top of each one. Divide the diced tomatoes among the fish fillets and wrap the spinach leaves over to enclose them completely.

3 Carefully transfer the spinach-wrapped fish to an ovenproof dish, arranging them in a single layer. Put on a baking sheet and bake for 10 to 15 minutes, or until the flesh flakes easily when tested with the point of a knife. Serve immediately, drizzled with extra virgin olive oil, if using.

Normandy Cream Mussels

INGREDIENTS

main

4½ lb/2 kg live mussels

1¼ cups hard cider

6 shallots, finely chopped

6 tbsp heavy cream

pantry

pepper

serves ④

1 Scrub the mussels under cold running water, scraping off any barnacles with a knife, and pull off the beards. Discard any mussels with broken shells or open ones that do not shut immediately when tapped sharply with the handle of a knife.

2 Pour the cider into an ovenproof casserole dish, add the shallots, and season with pepper. Bring to a boil and cook for 2 minutes.

3 Add the mussels, cover with a tight-fitting lid, and cook over high heat, shaking the casserole dish occasionally, for about 5 minutes until the shells have opened. Remove the mussels with a slotted spoon, discarding any that remain closed, and keep warm.

4 Strain the cooking liquid through a cheesecloth-lined strainer into a pan. Bring to a boil and cook for 8 to 10 minutes until reduced by about half. Stir in the cream and add the mussels. Cook for 1 minute to reheat the shellfish, then serve in warmed bowls.

Mussels with Garlic & Parsley Butter

INGREDIENTS

serves 4

main

3 large garlic cloves

¾ cup unsalted butter, softened

2 oz/55 g fresh parsley, chopped

4½ lb/2 kg live mussels

pantry

salt and pepper

1 Place the garlic cloves on a board and flatten with the blade of a knife. Add a large pinch of salt and crush to a paste. Beat the paste into the butter in a bowl, add the parsley and season with pepper. Shape into a cylinder, wrap in wax paper, and chill in the refrigerator.

2 Scrub the mussels under cold running water, and pull off the beards. Discard any broken shells or open ones that do not shut immediately when tapped sharply with the handle of a knife.

3 Preheat the broiler. Push the tip of a small sharp knife between each mussel shell on the straight side. Run the knife around between the shells, then ease back the top shell. Run the knife around the inside edge of the top shell, pull it back and snap it off.

4 Arrange the half shells in a single layer in an ovenproof dish. Dot the mussel flesh with the butter. Cook under the broiler for 5 to 8 minutes, or until the mussels are lightly browned and the butter has melted. Serve immediately.

Scallops in Vermouth

INGREDIENTS

main

2 lb/1 kg shelled fresh scallops

4 tbsp unsalted butter

4 tbsp Noilly Prat or other dry vermouth

3 tbsp chopped fresh flat-leaf parsley

pantry

salt and pepper

serves ❹

1 If necessary, rinse the scallops and pat dry with paper towels. Season them with salt and pepper.

2 Melt 1 tablespoon of the butter in a large skillet. When it's just beginning to color, add half the scallops and cook, turning occasionally, for 4 to 5 minutes until light golden brown on both sides. Remove from the skillet and keep warm. Melt another 1 tablespoon of the butter in the skillet and cook the remaining scallops in the same way, then remove them from the skillet and keep warm.

3 Add the Noilly Prat to the skillet and stir in the remaining butter. When it has melted, stir in the parsley and pour the sauce over the scallops. Serve immediately, seasoned with pepper.

Mustard Shrimp

INGREDIENTS

main

20–24 raw jumbo shrimp

4 tbsp unsalted butter

1 cup heavy cream

1 tbsp Dijon mustard

pantry

salt and pepper

serves ❹

1 Pull off the heads from the shrimp and peel them. Make an incision along the back of each shrimp with a small sharp knife and carefully remove the dark black vein with the point of the knife.

2 Melt the butter in a large skillet, add the shrimp, and cook, stirring frequently, for 3 to 4 minutes. Pour in the cream, season with salt and pepper, and stir in the mustard. Simmer gently over low heat for an additional 5 minutes. Serve immediately.

Shrimp in Orange Juice

INGREDIENTS

main

3 red bell peppers

30–36 large raw shrimp

2 tbsp olive oil

juice of 1 large orange

pantry

salt and pepper

serves 6

1 Preheat the broiler. Put the peppers on a baking sheet and cook under the broiler, turning frequently, until the skins are blistered and charred. Using tongs, transfer to a plastic bag, tie the top, and leave until cool enough to handle.

2 Meanwhile, pull off the heads from the shrimp and peel them. Make an incision along the back of each shrimp with a small sharp knife and carefully remove the dark black vein with the point of the knife.

3 When the peppers are cool enough to handle, peel off the skins, then halve and seed them. Cut the flesh into thin strips.

4 Heat the oil in a large skillet, add the pepper strips, season with salt and pepper, cover, and cook over low heat, for 5 minutes. Add the shrimp and cook, stirring occasionally, for 3 to 4 minutes, then pour in the orange juice and simmer for an additional 2 to 3 minutes until the shrimp are tender. Taste and adjust the seasoning, if necessary, and serve.

Hot Chile Shrimp

INGREDIENTS

main

3–4 fresh green chiles

juice of 1 lime

2 tbsp peanut oil

24 raw jumbo shrimp

pantry

pepper

serves 6

1 Seed the chiles if you prefer a milder flavor, then chop coarsely. Put the chiles, lime juice, and oil in a food processor and process until thoroughly combined. Pour the mixture into a nonmetallic dish.

2 Pull off the heads from the shrimp and peel them. Make an incision along the back of each shrimp with a small sharp knife and carefully remove the dark black vein with the point of the knife. Add the shrimp to the dish and stir to coat. Cover with plastic wrap and let marinate for 30 minutes.

3 Preheat the broiler. Drain the shrimp, reserving the marinade, and thread them onto 6 skewers. Cook under the broiler, turning frequently and brushing with the marinade, for 5 minutes, until tender. Alternatively, you can cook the shrimp on the barbecue. Serve immediately, seasoned with pepper.

3 Meat & Poultry

Whether special-occasion dishes with the choicest cuts, or inexpensive family suppers based on more economical meats, these fabulous dishes are sure to please. It's hard to believe that tasty stews, braises, and roasts, spicy chicken, and fruity duck breasts simply result from the ingenious combination of just four ingredients.

Peppered Steak

INGREDIENTS

serves 4

main

4 tbsp green peppercorns

4 porterhouse steaks, about 8 oz/225 g each, trimmed

8 tbsp butter

2 tbsp brandy

1 Press the peppercorns into both sides of the steaks. Place on a plate, cover, and let stand for 1 hour.

2 Heat a large, heavy-bottom skillet, add the butter and, as soon as it has melted, add the steaks. Cook for 2 to 4 minutes on each side, until cooked to your liking. Remove the steaks with a spatula and keep warm.

3 Add the brandy to the skillet and stir well to mix. Spoon the sauce over the steaks and serve immediately.

Stuffed Beef Tenderloin

INGREDIENTS

main

**1 beef tenderloin, about
1½ lb/600 g**

**5 tbsp finely chopped
sundried tomatoes in oil**

**bunch of fresh mixed
herbs, finely chopped**

1 tbsp sunflower oil

serves ❹

1 Preheat the oven to 325°F/160°C. Using a ham knife, fish filleting knife, or other knife with a strong, thin blade, pierce the center of the beef from one side. Twist the knife in circles until you have drilled a tunnel about ½ inch/1 cm wide all the way through.

2 Mix the sundried tomatoes and herbs together in a bowl. Spoon the mixture into the tunnel, pushing it in with your fingers or the handle of a wooden spoon.

3 Heat the oil in an ovenproof casserole dish, add the beef, and cook over high heat, turning frequently, for 5 to 8 minutes, or until evenly browned on all sides. Transfer the casserole dish to the oven and roast, basting occasionally, for 20 to 25 minutes for rare beef, 30 to 35 minutes for medium rare, and 45 to 55 minutes for well done.

4 Remove the beef from the oven and let cool completely before slicing and serving.

Pork & Potatoes in Red Wine

INGREDIENTS

main

4 pork chops

1½ lb/700g waxy potatoes, cut into large pieces

1 tsp coriander seeds, crushed

1¾ cups red wine

pantry

salt and pepper

serves 4

1 Trim the fat from the chops and melt it in a nonstick skillet. Add the potatoes and cook over medium-low heat, stirring and turning occasionally, for 20 minutes until golden brown all over. Remove from the skillet with a slotted spoon and place in an ovenproof casserole dish.

2 Add the chops to the skillet and cook over medium heat, turning occasionally, for 8 to 10 minutes until evenly browned all over. Transfer to the casserole dish.

3 Gently stir the coriander seeds into the casserole dish, season with salt and pepper, and pour in the red wine. Bring to a boil, then reduce the heat, cover, and simmer for 40 minutes, or until the meat is tender. Serve immediately, straight from the casserole dish.

Lamb with Roquefort & Walnut Butter

INGREDIENTS

main

4 tbsp unsalted butter

5 oz/140 g Roquefort cheese, crumbled

2 tbsp finely chopped walnuts

8 lamb noisettes

pantry

salt and pepper

snipped chives, to garnish (optional)

serves 4

1 Cream half the butter in a bowl with a wooden spoon. Beat in the cheese and walnuts until thoroughly combined and season with salt and pepper to taste. Turn out the flavored butter onto a sheet of wax paper and shape into a cylinder. Wrap and let chill in the refrigerator until firm.

2 Heat a ridged grill pan, add the remaining butter, and as soon as it has melted, add the lamb noisettes. Then cook for 4 to 5 minutes on each side.

3 Transfer the lamb to warmed serving plates and top each noisette with a slice of Roquefort and walnut butter. Serve immediately with snipped chives, to garnish, if using.

Irish Stew

INGREDIENTS

main

3 lb/1.3 kg potatoes, peeled

2 lb/1 kg best end of neck or other stewing lamb, trimmed of fat

1 lb/500 g onions, thinly sliced

2 tbsp chopped fresh parsley

pantry

4 cups water

salt and pepper

serves 4 to 6

1 Thinly slice half the potatoes. Make alternating layers of lamb, onions, and sliced potatoes in a large pan, seasoning each layer with salt and pepper. Pour in the water so that the layers are just covered.

2 Bring to a boil, then reduce the heat, cover, and simmer gently for 1¾ hours. Cut the remaining potatoes into quarters and place on top of the stew to steam. Re-cover the pan and simmer for an additional 45 minutes, or until the potato quarters are tender.

3 Arrange the steamed potatoes around the outside of a warmed serving dish. Place the meat, onions, and sliced potatoes in the center. Taste the cooking liquid and adjust the seasoning, if necessary, then spoon it over the meat. Sprinkle with the parsley and serve immediately.

Greek Lamb Patties

INGREDIENTS

main

2 lb/1 kg ground lamb

1 onion, grated

½ tsp freshly grated nutmeg

1 cup pine nuts, coarsely chopped

pantry

salt and pepper

serves **4** to **6**

1 Preheat the broiler. Put all the ingredients in a bowl and season with salt and pepper. Mix thoroughly with your hands until combined, then shape into 12 patties.

2 Place the patties on a broiler rack and cook under the broiler for 8 minutes on each side until golden brown and cooked through. Serve immediately.

Bacon-Wrapped Sausages

INGREDIENTS

serves 4

main

8 pork sausages

2 tbsp mild mustard

24 ready-to-eat prunes

8 slices smoked bacon

1 Preheat the broiler. Using a sharp knife, cut a slit along the length of each sausage about three-quarters of the way through. Spread the mustard inside the slits and press 3 prunes into each sausage.

2 Stretch the bacon with the back of a knife until each slice is quite thin. Wrap a slice of bacon around each sausage.

3 Place the sausages on a broiler rack and cook under the broiler, turning occasionally, for 15 to 20 minutes until cooked through and browned all over. Serve immediately.

Tagliatelle with Ham

INGREDIENTS

main

1 lb/450 g fresh or dried tagliatelle

¾ cup unsalted butter

12 oz/350 g prosciutto, cut into 2-inch/5-cm strips

6 oz/175 g Parmesan cheese, grated

pantry

salt and pepper

serves 4

1 If you are using dried tagliatelle, cook it in a large pan of boiling salted water for 10 to 12 minutes, or until tender but still firm to the bite. If you are using fresh tagliatelle, it will be ready in 2 to 3 minutes after the water has come back to a boil.

2 Meanwhile, melt the butter in a skillet. Add the prosciutto and cook over medium heat, stirring continuously, for 5 minutes. Remove the skillet from the heat.

3 Drain the tagliatelle and tip it into a warmed serving dish. Add the prosciutto and melted butter and toss well. Sprinkle evenly with the grated Parmesan cheese, season with pepper, and serve.

Chicken Roll

INGREDIENTS

main

4 oz/115 g ground veal

4 skinless, boneless chicken breast portions, about 4½ oz/125 g each

1 cup Boursin or other cream cheese flavored with garlic and herbs

3 tbs honey

pantry

salt and pepper

fresh sage leaves, to garnish (optional)

serves ❹

1 Put the ground veal in a pan and cook over medium-low heat, stirring frequently, for 5 minutes until evenly browned and broken up. Season with salt and pepper and remove the skillet from the heat. Let cool.

2 Preheat the oven to 375°F/190°C. Spread out a sheet of plastic wrap and place the chicken portions on top, side by side. Cover with another sheet of plastic wrap and beat gently with a meat mallet until the portions form a continuous sheet about ½ inch/1 cm thick.

3 Remove the chicken from the plastic wrap and spread the cheese over one side of it. Spoon the ground veal evenly over the top. Roll up the chicken from one short side and brush with the honey.

4 Place the chicken roll in a roasting pan and cook for 1 hour, or until tender and cooked through. Transfer the chicken roll to a cutting board and cut into thin slices. Serve immediately garnished with sage leaves, if using.

Pan-Fried Chicken with Golden Sauce

INGREDIENTS

main

2 mangoes

14 oz/400 g canned apricots in juice

4 tbsp unsalted butter

4 skinless, boneless chicken breasts, about 6 oz/175 g each

pantry

salt and pepper

serves ❹

1 Using a sharp knife, slice off the sides of the mangoes as close to the seeds as possible. Cut through the flesh in the half shells in a criss-cross pattern, turn inside out, and cut off the flesh. Cut off any remaining flesh from the seeds. Place in a food processor.

2 Drain the apricots, setting aside about 1 cup of the can juice. Put the apricots and reserved juice into the food processor and process until smooth. Pour the sauce into a small pan.

3 Melt the butter in a large, heavy-bottom skillet. Add the chicken and cook over medium-low heat, turning occasionally, for 15 minutes until golden all over and cooked through. Test by piercing the thickest part with the point of a sharp knife. If the juices run clear, the chicken is cooked.

4 Meanwhile, place the pan of sauce over low heat to warm through, but not boil.

5 Slice the chicken portions diagonally and arrange on warmed serving plates. Spoon the sauce over them and serve immediately, seasoned with salt and pepper.

Chicken & Apricots

INGREDIENTS

main

¼ cup all-purpose flour

4 chicken portions

4 tbsp olive oil

2 cups dried apricots, soaked overnight in 2½ cups water

pantry

salt and pepper

serves ❹

1 Spread out the flour on a plate and season with salt and pepper. Roll the chicken portions in the flour to coat, shaking off any excess. Set aside the remaining seasoned flour.

2 Heat the oil in an ovenproof casserole dish, add the chicken, and cook over medium heat, turning occasionally, for 8 to 10 minutes until golden brown. Remove with a slotted spoon and set aside.

3 Drain the apricots, setting aside the soaking liquid. Add the reserved flour to the casserole dish and cook over low heat, stirring continuously, for 2 minutes. Gradually stir in the reserved soaking liquid and bring to the boil, while stirring continuously.

4 Add the apricots and return the chicken to the casserole dish. Cover and simmer gently for 45 minutes, or until the chicken is tender and cooked through. Test by piercing the thickest part with the point of a knife. If the juices run clear, the chicken is ready. Serve immediately.

Chicken in a Salt Crust

INGREDIENTS

main

**bunch of fresh
flat-leaf parsley**

**1 chicken, about
3½ lb/1.5 kg**

3½ lb/1.5 kg sea salt

1 egg white

pantry

fresh thyme sprigs, to garnish
(optional)

serves ❹

1 Preheat the oven to 350°F/180°C. Line a roasting pan, large enough to hold the chicken, with a double thickness of foil, letting it overhang the sides. Put the parsley in the cavity of the chicken and tie the legs with kitchen string.

2 Mix the sea salt and egg white together in a bowl until thoroughly combined and the salt is moist. Spoon a layer of the salt mixture into the prepared pan, spreading it out evenly. Place the chicken on top and cover with the remaining salt mixture to cover it completely.

3 Fold the hanging sides of foil over the chicken to enclose it completely and bake for 1½ hours.

4 Remove the chicken, still wrapped in foil, from the roasting pan. Open the foil and break the salt crust with the back of a large knife. Brush away all traces of salt and transfer the chicken to a carving board. Serve immediately garnished with thyme, if using.

Lemon Roast Chicken

INGREDIENTS

main

**1 chicken, about
3½ lb/1.5 kg**

**1 fresh bouquet garni or
6 fresh tarragon sprigs**

1 lemon

**heaping 1 tbsp unsalted
butter, softened**

pantry

5 tbsp water

salt and pepper

serves 4

1 Preheat the oven to 400°F/200°C. Place a rack in a roasting pan for the chicken.

2 Season the chicken inside and out with salt and pepper. Put the herbs in the cavity. Squeeze the juice from one half of the lemon into the cavity, then add the squeezed half. Tie the chicken legs with kitchen string.

3 Rub the butter over the chicken and transfer to the rack. Squeeze over the juice from the remaining lemon half. Roast for 1½ hours until cooked through and tender. Test by piercing the thickest part with the point of a knife. If the juices run clear, the chicken is cooked.

4 Remove the chicken from the pan, tent with foil, and let stand for 15 minutes. Remove the rack from the roasting pan.

5 Skim off the fat from the cooking juices with a metal spoon and place the pan over medium heat. Pour in the water and bring to a boil, stirring, and scraping any sediment from the bottom of the pan with a wooden spoon. Strain the gravy into a gravy-boat. Carve the chicken into slices and serve with the gravy.

Thai Chicken

INGREDIENTS

main

6 garlic cloves, coarsely chopped

8 chicken legs

1 tbsp Thai fish sauce

4 tbsp dark soy sauce

pantry

pepper

matchsticks of fresh ginger, to garnish (optional)

serves 4

1 Put the garlic cloves in a mortar, add 1 teaspoon of black pepper, and pound to a paste with a pestle. Using a sharp knife, make 3 to 4 diagonal slashes on both sides of the chicken legs. Spread the garlic paste over the chicken legs and place them in a dish. Add the fish sauce and soy sauce and turn the legs to coat well. Cover with plastic wrap and let marinate in the refrigerator for 2 hours.

2 Preheat the broiler. Drain the chicken legs, setting aside the marinade. Put them on a broiler rack and cook under the broiler, turning and basting frequently with the reserved marinade, for 20 to 25 minutes, or until cooked through and tender. Test by piercing the thickest part with the point of a knife. If the juices run clear, the chicken is cooked. Serve immediately garnished with matchsticks of ginger, if using.

Honeyed Duck with Grapefruit

INGREDIENTS

main

1 grapefruit

4 duck breast fillets

4 tbsp honey

**fresh thyme sprigs,
to garnish**

pantry

salt and pepper

serves 4

1 Preheat the broiler. Peel the grapefruit, removing all traces of the white pith. Using a small, sharp knife, cut out each segment between the membranes. Set aside.

2 Using a sharp knife, make 3 deep diagonal slashes on the skin side of the duck breasts. Brush the duck all over with honey and season with salt and pepper.

3 Place the duck breasts, skin-side down, in an ovenproof dish, and cook under the broiler for 2 minutes. Remove the dish from the broiler and turn the duck over. Put a grapefruit segment in each of the slashes, pressing it in firmly. Brush with the remaining honey and broil for an additional 3 minutes.

4 Serve the duck immediately, garnished with the thyme sprigs.

Deviled Turkey Legs

INGREDIENTS

main

2 turkey legs, skinned

½ tsp cayenne pepper

2 tbsp Dijon or hot mustard

3 tbsp unsalted butter, softened

pantry

salt and pepper

serves 4

1 Make deep criss-cross slashes in the turkey legs. Season with salt and pepper and sprinkle with a little of the cayenne pepper. Spread the mustard all over the legs, pressing it well into the slashes. Place the legs in a large, deep dish, cover with plastic wrap, and let marinate in the refrigerator for 6 to 8 hours.

2 Meanwhile, cream the butter in a bowl, then beat in the remaining cayenne pepper to taste. Cover the bowl with plastic wrap and leave until you are ready to serve.

3 Preheat the broiler. Place the turkey legs on a broiler rack and cook under the broiler, turning frequently, for 15 to 20 minutes, or until golden brown and cooked through. Test by inserting the point of a sharp knife in the thickest part. If the juices run clear, the turkey is cooked.

4 Transfer the turkey legs to a carving board and carve into slices. Arrange on a serving plate with the cayenne butter. Serve immediately.

4 Vegetables & Vegetarian Dishes

The recipes in this chapter include inspiring accompaniments, flavorsome vegetarian main courses and a tempting selection of salads. As well as an extensive range of vegetables, the recipes also feature eggs, cheese, pasta, and rice and many can be served on their own or mixed and matched with some of the dishes from earlier chapters.

Hot Roast Peppers

INGREDIENTS

serves 6

main

6 red bell peppers, seeded and cut into thick strips

5 oz/140 g fresh green serrano or jalapeño chiles, seeded and sliced into thin strips

2 garlic cloves, crushed

4 tbsp extra virgin olive oil

1 Preheat the oven to 400°F/200°C. Make alternating layers of bell peppers, chiles, and garlic in a shallow casserole dish. Pour in the olive oil.

2 Cover and bake for 50 to 60 minutes, or until the peppers have softened. Remove the lid and reduce the temperature to 350°F/180°C. Return the casserole dish to the oven and bake for an additional 45 minutes, or until the peppers are very soft and beginning to char.

3 Serve immediately if serving hot. Alternatively, let cool, then transfer to a large screw-top jar and store in the refrigerator for up to 3 weeks, topped off with more olive oil to keep the peppers covered, if necessary.

Tomato & Eggplant Layers

INGREDIENTS

main

3 tbsp olive oil

2 eggplants, thinly sliced

4 tomatoes, peeled and sliced

3 tbsp chopped fresh flat-leaf parsley

pantry

salt and pepper

serves 4

1 Preheat the oven to 375°F/190°C. Heat the oil in a large skillet, add the eggplant slices, in batches if necessary, and cook over medium-low heat, turning once or twice, for 4 minutes. Remove with a spatula.

2 Make alternating layers of tomato slices, parsley, and eggplant slices in a casserole dish, seasoning each layer with salt and pepper and ending with a layer of tomatoes.

3 Cover and bake for 1 hour, or until the vegetables are tender. Serve immediately.

Eggs in Potato Shells

INGREDIENTS

main

4 large baking potatoes

4 tbsp butter

2 tbsp light cream

4 eggs

pantry

salt and pepper

serves 4

1 Preheat the oven to 400°F/200°C. Prick the potatoes with a fork and bake for 1 hour, or until soft.

2 Remove the potatoes from the oven but do not switch the oven off. Cut each potato, lengthwise, in half and use a teaspoon to scoop out the flesh into a bowl, without piercing the shells. Mash the flesh with the butter and cream and season with salt and pepper.

3 Pile the mashed potato back into the shells and place them in an ovenproof dish that will hold them steady. Make a hollow in the center of each and break in an egg. Season with salt and pepper.

4 Put the dish in the oven and bake for 10 to 15 minutes, or until the eggs are just set. Then serve immediately.

Soufflé Cauliflower Cheese

INGREDIENTS

serves ❹

main

1½ lb/650 g cauliflower, cut into florets

4 eggs, separated

4 oz/115 g bleu cheese, crumbled

2 tsp Dijon mustard

pantry

salt and pepper

1 Preheat the oven to 375°F/190°C. Cook the cauliflower in a large pan of salted boiling water for 5 to 10 minutes, or until just tender. Drain well, refresh under cold running water, and drain again.

2 Put the cauliflower florets and egg yolks into a food processor and process until smooth and combined. Transfer the mixture to a bowl and stir in the cheese and mustard. Season with salt and pepper.

3 Whisk the egg whites in a grease-free bowl until stiff. Using a rubber spatula, gently fold about one-third of the egg whites into the cauliflower mixture. Fold in the remaining egg whites in 2 batches.

4 Transfer the mixture to individual soufflé dishes and bake for 35 minutes, or until well risen and golden brown on top. Serve immediately.

Mixed Potato Rösti

INGREDIENTS

main

11½ oz/325 g potatoes

11½ oz/325 g sweet potatoes

4 tbsp sunflower oil

3 tbsp butter

pantry

salt

serves 4

1 Parboil the ordinary potatoes in a large pan of salted water for 10 minutes, then drain and let cool. Meanwhile, peel and coarsely grate the sweet potatoes into a bowl. When the parboiled potatoes have cooled, peel and coarsely grate into another bowl.

2 Divide the potatoes and the sweet potatoes separately into 4 equal portions and shape each portion into a pattie about ½ inch/1 cm thick, pressing them together firmly.

3 Heat half the oil with half the butter in a heavy-bottom skillet. Add the potato rösti and cook over medium heat for 5 minutes, or until crisp and golden on the undersides. Turn them carefully with a spatula, pat into shape if necessary, and cook for an additional 5 minutes, or until golden brown on the second side. Remove from the skillet and keep warm.

4 Heat the remaining oil and butter in the skillet. Add the sweet potato rösti and cook for 5 minutes on each side as before. Remove from the pan and serve both types of potato rösti immediately.

Pasta with Tomatoes & Spinach

INGREDIENTS

main

1 lb/450 g dried orecchiette or other pasta shapes

3 tbsp olive oil

8 oz/225 g fresh baby spinach leaves, tough stalks removed

1 lb/450 g cherry tomatoes, halved

pantry

salt and pepper

Parmesan cheese, grated (optional)

serves 4

1 Cook the pasta in a large pan of boiling salted water for 10 to 12 minutes, or until tender but still firm to the bite.

2 Heat the oil in a pan, add the spinach and tomatoes, and cook, gently stirring occasionally, for 2 to 3 minutes, or until the spinach has wilted and the tomatoes are heated through but not disintegrating.

3 Drain the pasta and add it to the pan of vegetables. Toss gently, season with salt and pepper, sprinkle over some Parmesan cheese if using, and serve immediately.

Spaghetti with Parsley & Parmesan

INGREDIENTS

serves ❹

main

1 lb/450 g dried spaghetti

¾ cup unsalted butter

4 tbsp chopped fresh flat-leaf parsley

8 oz/225 g Parmesan cheese, grated

pantry

salt

1 Cook the pasta in a large pan of boiling salted water for 10 to 12 minutes, or until tender but still firm to the bite. Drain and tip into a warmed serving dish.

2 Add the butter, parsley, and half the Parmesan cheese and toss well, using 2 forks, until the butter and cheese have melted. Serve immediately with the remaining Parmesan cheese handed separately.

Leeks with Cheese & Eggs

INGREDIENTS

main

6 tbsp unsalted butter

8 leeks, trimmed

6 tbsp freshly grated Parmesan cheese

4 eggs

pantry

salt and pepper

serves **4**

1 Preheat the oven to 325°F/160°C. Grease an ovenproof dish with a little of the butter.

2 Bring a large pan of salted water to a boil, add the leeks, and cook for 7 to 10 minutes, or until tender but still firm to the bite. Drain well and carefully squeeze out as much water as possible. Pat dry with paper towels.

3 Place the leeks in the prepared dish. Sprinkle with half the Parmesan cheese and dot with one-third of the remaining butter. Bake in the oven for 5 minutes.

4 Meanwhile, melt the remaining butter in a skillet. Add the eggs, one at a time, and cook until the whites are just set. Remove the leeks from the oven and, using a spatula, top with the eggs. Pour the butter from the pan over them, sprinkle with the remaining Parmesan cheese, and season with pepper. Serve immediately.

Cheese & Vegetable Tart

INGREDIENTS

main

12 oz/350 g prepared, unsweetened pie dough, thawed if frozen

10 oz/280 g mixed frozen vegetables

⅔ cup heavy cream

4 oz/115 g cheddar cheese, grated

pantry

salt and pepper

serves ❹

1 Thinly roll out the dough on a lightly floured counter and use to line a 9-inch/23-cm tart pan. Prick the base and chill in the refrigerator for 30 minutes. Preheat the oven to 400°F/200°C.

2 Line the pastry shell with foil and half-fill with dried beans. Place the pan on a baking sheet and bake for 15 to 20 minutes, or until just firm. Remove the beans and foil, return the pastry shell to the oven, and bake for an additional 5 to 7 minutes until golden. Remove the pastry shell from the oven and let cool in the pan.

3 Meanwhile, cook the frozen vegetables in a pan of salted boiling water. Drain and let cool.

4 When ready to cook, preheat the oven again to 400°F/200°C. Mix the cooked vegetables and cream together and season with salt and pepper. Spoon the mixture evenly into the pastry shell and sprinkle with the cheese. Bake for 15 minutes, or until the cheese has melted and is turning golden. Serve hot or cold.

Mexican Rice

INGREDIENTS

serves 4

main

1 onion, chopped

14 oz/400 g plum tomatoes, peeled, seeded, and chopped

1 cup beef stock

1 cup long-grain rice

pantry

salt and pepper

1 Put the onion and tomatoes in a food processor and process to a smooth purée. Scrape the purée into a pan, pour in the stock, and bring to a boil over medium heat, stirring occasionally.

2 Add the rice and stir once, then reduce the heat, cover, and simmer for 20 to 25 minutes until all the liquid has been absorbed and the rice is tender. Season with salt and pepper to taste and serve immediately.

Tomatoes with Goat Cheese

INGREDIENTS

main

12 tomatoes

6 round goat cheeses, about 1½ oz/40 g each

3 fresh basil sprigs, chopped

1 egg, lightly beaten

pantry

salt and pepper

serves ❻

1 Slice the tops off the tomatoes at the stalk end and set aside. Scoop out the flesh and seeds with a teaspoon, taking care not to pierce the tomato shells. Discard the tomato seeds and put the flesh into a bowl. Sprinkle the inside of each tomato shell with a pinch of salt, turn upside down on paper towels, and let drain for 45 minutes.

2 Add the cheese and basil to the tomato flesh in the bowl and mash well until thoroughly combined. Season with salt and pepper and beat in the egg until the mixture is thick and sticky.

3 Preheat the oven to 325°F/160°C. Spoon the cheese mixture into the tomato shells and replace the lids. Put the tomatoes in an ovenproof dish that will hold them securely and bake for 10 minutes. Turn off the oven but do not remove the tomatoes for 5 minutes, then serve.

Moroccan Tomato & Red Pepper Salad

INGREDIENTS

serves 4

main

3 red bell peppers

4 ripe tomatoes

1/2 bunch of fresh cilantro, chopped

2 garlic cloves, finely chopped

pantry

salt and pepper

1 Preheat the broiler. Place the bell peppers on a baking sheet and cook under the broiler, turning occasionally, for 15 minutes. Add the tomatoes and broil, turning occasionally, for an additional 5 to 10 minutes, or until all the skins are charred and blistered. Remove from the heat and let cool.

2 Peel and seed the bell peppers and tomatoes and slice the flesh thinly. Place in a bowl, mix well, and season with salt and pepper. Sprinkle with the cilantro and garlic, cover with plastic wrap, and chill in the refrigerator for at least 1 hour. Just before serving, drain off any excess liquid.

Onion & Orange Salad

INGREDIENTS

main

4 oranges

2 white onions, thinly sliced and pushed out into rings

16 black olives, pitted

extra virgin olive oil, for drizzling

pantry

salt and pepper

serves ❹

1 Peel the oranges, removing all traces of bitter white pith. Using a sharp knife, cut the flesh crosswise into slices and remove the seeds, if necessary.

2 Arrange the orange slices and onion rings in concentric circles on individual serving plates and season with salt and pepper. Place 4 olives in the center of each plate and drizzle the salads with olive oil. Cover and let stand for 30 minutes before serving.

Tomato & Feta Salad

INGREDIENTS

main

2 lb/1 kg ripe tomatoes, thickly sliced

8 oz/225 g feta cheese

½ cup extra virgin olive oil

16 black olives, pitted

pantry

pepper

serves ❹

1 Arrange the tomato slices in concentric rings on a serving dish. Crumble the feta over the tomatoes and drizzle with the olive oil. Top with the olives.

2 Season to taste with pepper. Salt is probably not necessary because feta is already quite salty. Let stand for 30 minutes before serving.

Mushroom Salad

INGREDIENTS

main

**8 oz/225 g white or pink
cremini mushrooms,
thinly sliced**

**finely grated rind and juice
of ½ lemon**

3 tbsp sour cream

1 tbsp chopped fresh chervil

pantry

salt and pepper

serves ❹

1 Put the mushrooms in a large bowl, sprinkle with the lemon rind and juice, and toss well. Gently stir in the sour cream and season with salt and pepper.

2 Cover the bowl with plastic wrap and let stand, stirring once or twice, for 1 hour. Spoon the salad into a serving bowl, sprinkle with the chervil, and serve.

5 Desserts

For many people a meal is not complete
without a sweet treat at the end, although
this sometimes seems a course too far
for the busy cook. Now, using just four
ingredients, you can whisk up irresistible
cold creamy desserts, mouthwatering hot
desserts, and even fabulous homemade
ices with little effort and superb results.

Layered Nectarine Cream

INGREDIENTS

main

4 nectarines, peeled, pitted, and sliced

2 tbsp amaretto liqueur

¾ cup curd cheese

1¼ cups peach-flavored yogurt

serves 4

1 Set aside a few nectarine slices for decoration. Put the remainder in a bowl, add the liqueur, and toss gently, then set aside.

2 Beat the cheese and yogurt together in another bowl until thoroughly combined. Spoon half the mixture into 4 tall glasses. Divide the nectarine and liqueur mixture among them and top with the remaining cheese and yogurt mixture.

3 Decorate with the reserved nectarine slices and let chill in the refrigerator for at least 30 minutes before serving.

Summer Dessert

INGREDIENTS

serves 6

main

2 lb/900 g mixed berries, such as raspberries and blackberries

¾ cup superfine sugar

½ cup milk

8 slices day-old white bread, crusts removed

1 Hull the berries and put them in a bowl. Sprinkle with the sugar and set aside.

2 Sprinkle the milk over the slices of bread to soften them slightly. Line the base and sides of an ovenproof bowl with two-thirds of the bread, cutting it to fit but overlap the edges slightly. Spoon the berries into the bowl and place the remaining bread slices on top, cutting to fit and making sure that the fruit is completely covered.

3 Place a circle of wax paper on top of the last layer of bread. Put a plate or saucer, slightly smaller than the diameter of the bowl, on top, then place a weight, such as a heavy can of fruit, on the plate. Let chill in the refrigerator for at least 8 hours.

4 To serve, remove the weight, plate, and wax paper. Invert a serving dish on top of the bowl and, holding them together, reverse and shake sharply and the dessert should slide out.

Honey & Chocolate Bananas

INGREDIENTS

main

4 tbsp unsalted butter

4 ripe bananas, peeled and halved lengthwise

4 tbsp honey

6 oz/175 g semisweet chocolate, grated

serves 4

1 Melt the butter in a skillet, add the bananas, and cook over medium-low heat, turning occasionally, for 4 to 5 minutes. Carefully transfer them to individual serving plates.

2 Drizzle 1 tablespoon of honey along the length of each banana and sprinkle with the grated chocolate. Serve immediately.

Pears in Wine

INGREDIENTS

serves ❹

main

4 large pears

heaping 1 cup superfine sugar

1 cinnamon stick or vanilla bean

⅔ cup red wine

pantry

⅔ cup water

1 Peel the pears, leaving the stalks intact. Cut a thin slice off the base of each pear so that it will stand upright.

2 Put the sugar and cinnamon stick in a large pan, add the water, and bring to a boil over medium heat, stirring until the sugar has dissolved. Add the pears, reduce the heat, cover, and then simmer for 15 minutes.

3 Pour in the wine and simmer, uncovered, for an additional 15 minutes, or until the pears are just tender. Remove the pears with a slotted spoon and stand them in a serving dish.

4 Remove and discard the cinnamon stick and bring the wine syrup back to a boil. Boil rapidly until thickened, then pour the syrup over the pears and let cool. Chill for at least 1 hour before serving.

Raspberries and Meringue Cream

INGREDIENTS

main

1 lb/500 g raspberries

4 tbsp amaretto or crème de framboise liqueur

1¼ cups heavy cream

6 small white meringues, coarsely crushed

serves ❹

1 Hull the raspberries, put them in a bowl, and sprinkle the liqueur over them. Cover with plastic wrap and let chill in the refrigerator for 2 hours.

2 Whisk the cream in a large bowl until soft peaks form, then fold the raspberries, with their juices, into it. Sprinkle the crushed meringues on top and gently fold in. Spoon into a serving dish and serve immediately.

Citrus Granita

INGREDIENTS

main

6 oranges

1½ lemons

¾ cup sugar

6 amaretti cookies

pantry

2 cups water

serves 6

1 Pare the rind from the fruit, then cut off and discard the pith. Slice a few thin strips of rind and put them to one side, separately from the large pieces. Squeeze the juice from the fruit.

2 Boil the sugar and water in a heavy-bottom pan and stir until the sugar dissolves. Boil, without stirring, for 10 minutes until syrupy. Remove from the heat, stir in the large rind pieces, cover, and let cool.

3 Strain the cooled syrup into a freezerproof container and stir in the juice. Freeze, uncovered, for 4 hours until slushy.

4 Blanch the thin rind strips in a pan of boiling water for 2 minutes. Drain and refresh with cold water. Pat dry with paper towels.

5 Remove the granita from the freezer and break up with a fork. Freeze again for an additional 4 hours until hard.

6 Remove the granita from the freezer and leave until slightly softened. Beat with a fork, then spoon into glasses and decorate with the rind strips. Serve with the cookies.

Black Currant Sherbet

INGREDIENTS

main

½ cup superfine sugar

1 lb/500 g black currants

2 tbsp lemon juice

1 tbsp egg white

pantry

½ cup water

serves 6

1 Boil the water and sugar in a pan, stirring until the sugar dissolves. Boil, without stirring, for an additional 2 minutes, then remove from the heat and let cool.

2 Put the black currants and lemon juice in a food processor and process to a purée. Add the cooled syrup and process to combine. Using a spatula, press the purée through a nylon strainer over a bowl to remove the seeds.

3 Pour the purée into a freezerproof container, cover with plastic wrap, and freeze for 3 to 4 hours until slushy. Remove from the freezer, chop up, and process until smooth. Add the egg white and process until combined.

4 Return the sherbet to the container, re-cover, and re-freeze for an additional 4 hours, or until almost firm. Remove from the freezer, chop up, and process until the sherbet is smooth.

5 Return the sherbet to the container, cover tightly, and return to the freezer, where it will keep for up to 5 days. Remove the sherbet from the freezer and let stand at room temperature to soften slightly before serving.

Sweet & Sour Fruit Compote

INGREDIENTS

main

1½ lb/650 g rhubarb, cut into 1-inch/2.5-cm pieces

juice of 2 oranges

⅓ cup vanilla sugar or superfine sugar, plus extra to serve

10 oz/280 g strawberries

serves ❹

1 Put the rhubarb in a pan, add the orange juice and sugar, and bring to a boil, stirring gently, until the sugar has dissolved. Reduce the heat and simmer, stirring occasionally, for 5 minutes.

2 Meanwhile, hull the strawberries and halve any large ones. Add them to the pan and simmer for an additional 5 minutes.

3 Divide the warm compote among individual serving bowls and serve immediately or let cool to room temperature. Sprinkle with extra sugar before serving.

Lime Snow

INGREDIENTS

main

3 limes

¼ cup superfine sugar

1 tbsp powdered gelatin

2 egg whites

pantry

1 cup water

serves ❹

1 Finely grate the rind of one lime. Set aside about one-quarter for decoration and put the remainder in a bowl. Squeeze the juice from all the limes and add to the bowl.

2 Put the sugar in a pan, pour in the water, and bring to a boil, stirring until the sugar has dissolved. Remove from the heat and sprinkle the gelatin over the liquid. Leave for 5 minutes, then swirl until the gelatin has dissolved completely. Pour the mixture into the bowl of lime juice, in a thin continuous stream, stirring continuously. Refrigerate for 30 minutes until beginning to set.

3 Whisk the egg whites in a grease-free bowl until stiff. Remove the lime mixture from the refrigerator and beat until it is foamy. Gently fold in the egg whites with a spatula in 2 batches. Return the mixture to the refrigerator and chill for an additional 15 minutes.

4 Remove the lime snow from the refrigerator and beat until light and fluffy. Divide among dishes and refrigerate for 2 to 3 hours. Sprinkle with the remaining rind before serving.

Chestnut Cream with Madeira

INGREDIENTS

main

6 trifle sponge cakes

¾ cup Madeira

12 oz/350 g canned sweetened chestnut purée

1 cup heavy cream

serves ❻

1 Place a trifle sponge in each of 6 glasses, trimming it to fit if necessary. Spoon the Madeira over the sponges and let stand for 15 minutes.

2 Divide the chestnut purée among the glasses and smooth the surface with the back of a spoon. If necessary, wipe the rims of the glasses with damp paper towels.

3 Whisk the cream in a bowl until stiff, then spoon into a pastry bag fitted with a star-shaped tip. Pipe the cream decoratively over the chestnut purée. Then let chill in the refrigerator for at least 30 minutes before serving.

Apricot Swirl

INGREDIENTS

main

14 oz/400 g canned apricots in fruit juice, drained

1 tbsp amaretto or Cointreau liqueur

¾ cup thick sour cream

2 tbsp chopped pistachios

serves ❹

1 Put the apricots and liqueur in a food processor and process to a purée. Put alternating spoonfuls of the purée and sour cream into 4 glasses, swirling them together gently to create marbling.

2 Sprinkle the pistachios over the top to decorate and serve immediately. Alternatively, let chill in the refrigerator for 30 to 45 minutes before serving.

Baked Apples with Ginger

INGREDIENTS

main

3 tbsp unsalted butter, plus extra for greasing

4 large baking apples

4 tbsp plum jam

3 tbsp chopped preserved ginger

pantry

1¼ cups water

serves ❹

1 Preheat the oven to 375°F/190°C. Grease a shallow ovenproof dish, large enough to hold all the apples steady, with butter.

2 Using an apple corer, core the apples without cutting all the way through to the base. Peel the top half of each. Using a sharp knife, enlarge the cavity slightly. Place the apples in the prepared dish.

3 Mix the plum jam and preserved ginger together in a bowl and spoon the mixture into the cavities. Melt the butter and brush it over the top halves of the apples. Spoon the remainder over the top of the filling.

4 Pour the water into the dish but not over the apples and bake, basting occasionally with the cooking juices, for 45 to 60 minutes. Serve.

Melon & Morello Cherries

INGREDIENTS

main

2 ogen melons

14–15 oz/400–425 g canned morello cherries, drained

2 tbsp kirsch

2 cups peach sherbet or flavor of your choice

serves ❹

1 Halve the melons horizontally and scoop out the seeds with a spoon. Using a melon baller, scoop out the flesh, leaving shells about ¼ inch/5 mm thick. Set the shells aside, put the melon balls in a bowl and chill in the refrigerator for 1 hour.

2 Meanwhile, mix the cherries and kirsch together in another bowl. Cover with plastic wrap and let macerate for 1 hour.

3 Add the chilled melon to the cherry mixture. Using the melon baller, scoop the sherbet into balls and add to the fruit mixture. Stir well, divide the mixture among the melon shells and serve immediately.